OUT OF THE PAST

AMISH TRADITION AND FAITH

MARY ANN McDONALD

SMITHMARK

DEDICATION
For my husband, Joe, the love of my life.

FURTHER READING

Good, Merle. *Who Are the Amish?* Intercourse, PA: Good Books, 1985.

Good, Merle and Phyllis. *20 Most Asked Questions about the Amish and Mennonites.* Lancaster, PA: Good Books, 1979.

Hostetler, John A. *Amish Roots: A Treasury of History, Wisdom, and Lore.* Baltimore: Johns Hopkins University Press, 1989, 2nd ed. 1992.

Israel, Fred L. *Meet the Amish.* New York: Chelsea House Publishers, 1986.

Kraybill, Donald B. *The Riddle of Amish Culture.* Baltimore: Johns Hopkins University Press, 1989, 3rd printing 1991.

Nolt, Steven M. *The History of The Amish.* Intercourse, PA: Good Books, 1992.

Seitz, Ruth Hoover. *Amish Ways.* Harrisburg, PA: RB Books, 1991.

Stone, Lynn M. *Pennsylvania Dutch Country.* Vero Beach, FL: Rourke Corporation, 1993.

Yoder, Joseph W. *Rosanna of the Amish.* Scottsdale, PA: Herald Press, 16th printing 1989.

Yoder, Joseph W. *Rosanna's Boys.* Harrisonburg, VA: Choice Productions, 1948, revised ed. 1987.

This edition published by Smithmark Publishers, a division of U.S. Media Holdings, Inc.,
16 East 32nd Street, New York, NY 10016

SMITHMARK books are available for bulk purchase for sales promotion and premium use.
For details write or call the manager of special sales,
SMITHMARK Publishers,
16 East 32nd Street, New York, NY 10016;
(212) 532-6600.

This book was designed and produced by Todtri Productions Limited
P.O. Box 572, New York, NY 10116-0572
FAX: (212) 279-1241

Printed and bound in Singapore

Library of Congress Catalog Card Number 95-070269
ISBN 0-8317-8169-6

Author: Mary Ann McDonald

Publisher: Robert Tod
Book Designer: Mark Weinberg
Production Coordinator: Heather Weigel
Project Editor: Edward Douglas
Editors: Linda Greer, Don Kennison
Typesetting: Command-O, NYC

PHOTO CREDITS

Bullaty Lomeo 11, 12-13, 16 (top), 24-25, 39, 44, 45, 87 (bottom), 91 (bottom), 107 (bottom), 108 (top & bottom), 116 (top), 122, 123, 125, 126-27

Sonja Bullaty 16 (bottom), 32–33, 38, 43 (top)

Irvin G. Hoover 18-19, 23 (top), 36-37, 40-41, 46 (top), 50–51, 51 (right), 56-57, 62 (top), 66-67, 68, 70, 71 (top & bottom), 72-73, 75, 84, 92 (left), 92-93, 99, 100-101, 102 (top & bottom), 103, 104-105

Patti McConville 27, 58 (top), 113 (right), 119 (top)

Joe McDonald 7, 17, 28-29, 31, 47, 59, 60-61, 64-65, 79, 86, 94-95

Mary Ann McDonald 26

New England Stock Photo
Jean Higgins 22, 58 (bottom), 107 (top), 109
Andre Jenny 82 (top), 124 (bottom)
Leonard C. Lacue 53
Brent Parrett 90
Jim Schwabel 43 (bottom), 118
Michael Sheldock 87 (top)
W. J. Talarowski 78
Jeremy Woodhouse 23 (bottom), 63, 85, 98 (bottom)

Photo Network
Esbin-Anderson 110
Michael Philip Manheim 114 (bottom), 120-121
D. & I. McDonald 97

Photolink
Jeff Greenberg 54, 112-113

Picture Perfect
Cy Furlan 20, 42

Terry Wild Studio 8-9, 29 (bottom), 34, 35, 52, 116 (bottom)

Unicorn Stock Photo
Andre Jenny 74, 76, 83, 88-89
Gerry Schnieders 91 (top)

John B. Willetts 4-5, 10, 14, 15, 21, 30, 46 (bottom), 62 (bottom), 77, 80-81, 98 (top), 114 (top), 115

Woodfin Camp & Associates
Alexandra Avakian 48, 49, 55, 106, 119 (bottom), 124 (top)
Maxim Engel 96 (bottom), 111, 117
Olivier Rebbot 69
Roger Werth 82 (bottom), 96 (top)

CONTENTS

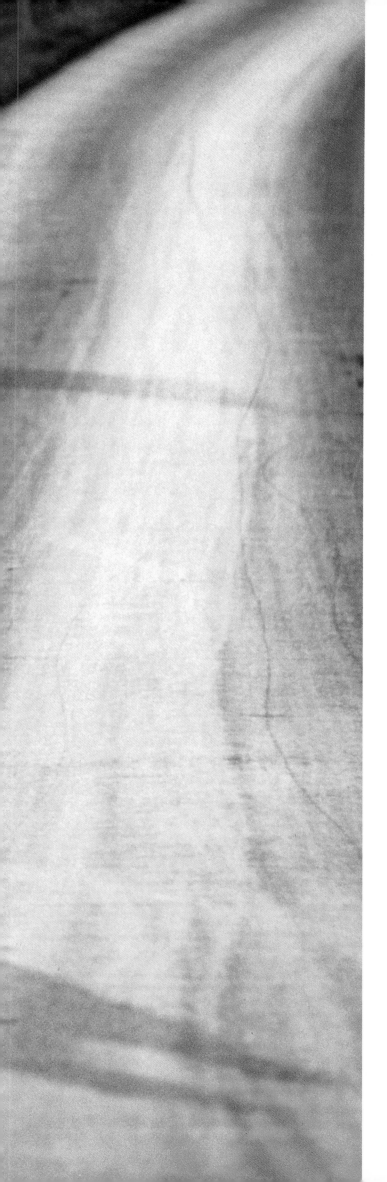

PREFACE

This book will discuss the lifestyle and beliefs of the Old Order Amish. For the sake of convenience, I will refer to them in the text simply as Amish. Throughout the book I will refer specifically to other religious sects with common Anabaptist roots, such as the Old Order Mennonites, New Order Amish, Hutterites, Church of the Brethren, Mennonites, and other Amish groups like the Nebraska and Beachy sects. These references will describe the differences between Amish sects and other groups.

It is very difficult to make definite statements about such cultural aspects as the dress of the people or the modernization of farms, since differences abound among the Amish. Whenever possible, I will make generalities regarding most of their practices and comparisons between the groups. The only constant among the Amish is their religious beliefs and practices, since many of these originated with the European founding fathers and have transcended time and place.

Living in Pennsylvania, I've been exposed to, and have been friends with, Amish people my entire life. My own ancestry runs deep in the Anabaptist movement, with my Mennonite ancestors arriving in the New World in 1722 and settling in Lancaster County. Many of my early ancestors were instrumental in the growth of the German Baptist Brethren church (known as the "Dunkers" and today as the Church of the Brethren). Although I live in the modern world, many of my beliefs and religious practices are similar to those of the Amish. I hope this book will help clarify any misconceptions and myths regarding this very dynamic, humble, and reverent people.

Left:
Two women walk home after a day of visiting. Roads in Amish country become polished by buggy wheels. At certain times of the year, the yellowish glow of the setting sun causes these roads to shimmer with a beautiful golden color.

INTRODUCTION

In today's society, the words *discipline, humility, sacrifice, faith, belief in God, brotherhood,* and *community* are seldom spoken, it seems, let alone adhered to. In the close-knit society of the Amish, these words are not only consistently spoken but govern every aspect of these people's daily lives. Criticized at times for their non-conformity and misunderstood for their beliefs, the Amish portray to the casual observer an image of quiet solitude, sternness, hypocrisy, and backwardness.

This impression is a false one, for the Amish live an existence steeped in tradition, basing their actions on the word of God and displaying to themselves and to others that the path to salvation is through deeds, and not simply with words. By living close to nature and nurturing the good Earth that God has given them, the Amish can truly be considered "stewards of the land."

EUROPEAN HISTORY

The Amish trace their ancestry back to the European Protestant Reformation of the early 1500s. Martin Luther and Ulrich Zwingli were two great leaders in the early days of the Protestant revolt; both rejected many of the doctrines of the Catholic Church and established the idea of separation of church and state.

Almost immediately, there were splinter groups within the ranks of these new reformers. Among some of Zwingli's followers in Zurich was a small radical group led by Konrad Grebel. This group believed that the church should be comprised of a body of adults who are voluntarily baptized when they are ready to commit themselves to a strict life of obedience as instructed by the words of Jesus Christ. These radicals soon became known as Anabaptists, meaning "rebaptizers," since the members had already been baptized as children in the Catholic Church.

In 1527, two years after the initial baptisms, the first leaders wrote a statement that solidified the beliefs and daily practices for the upstart church. These beliefs—voluntary adult baptism, separation of state and church, excommunication of errant individuals from communion, strict adherence to the Scriptures of the New Testament, and a life of nonviolence—are still the foundation of many groups today.

As the Anabaptist movement became more active and spread throughout Switzerland, Germany, and the Netherlands, so did the persecution of its followers. Condemned by both the church of Rome and the Protestant church, the "Brethren," as they referred to themselves, were subjected to years of torture, burning at the stake, drowning, and imprisonment. Within a few years many of the leaders were killed, but the movement thrived. In northern Europe, a Dutch priest who left the Catholic Church in 1536 after years of conflict emerged as one of the strongest leaders of the fractured Anabaptists. Menno Simons became so influential in the Anabaptist movement that his followers were called Mennonists, or Mennonites.

During the next 150 years, the Anabaptist community would split many times. In 1693 Jacob Ammann, a young Anabaptist leader from the Alsace region of France, grew worried that the purity of the church was in jeopardy. He wanted to introduce the practice of holding communion twice a year instead of only once, and he believed that foot washing should be incorporated into the communion service as a rite demonstrating true humility.

Ammann was also more strictly disciplined in dress and the trimming of beards, but the issue that finally widened the chasm beyond repair was that of "shunning" excommunicated members. He believed in the total exclusion of the castigated member from both communion and social contacts; this was the only way, he believed, for the church to remain pure and for the brotherhood to survive. The followers of Ammann became known as the Amish.

EMIGRATION TO AMERICA

In 1682 William Penn founded Penn's Woods, or Pennsylvania. Penn, who had converted to Quakerism, was himself persecuted in England for his beliefs. After his release from incarceration in the Tower of London he convinced Charles II to grant him a huge tract of land in the New World in exchange for a claim Penn's father held against the British treasury. With this land he established a colony where religious freedom was the order for anyone seeking it.

Advertising throughout Europe, he attracted many groups to his new settlement, including Quakers,

Right:
As dusk approaches, an Amish buggy heads for home. A common silhouette along the horizon in certain areas, this has become the symbol of the Amish people to the outside world. The buggy represents a simple way of life and the rejection of the modern world and all its entrapments.

Next in the hierarchy is the minister, whose main role is that of preacher and counselor. The deacon's responsibilities include the reading of the Scriptures and the second prayer during church services, administering financial aid to needy members, assisting in church discipline, and aiding the bishop with baptisms and communion. Most importantly, the deacon is a key figure in marriage arrangements.

All church leaders are chosen by lot. When either a deacon's or a minister's position becomes vacant, the church members select the applicants. After being counseled by the bishop on the importance of the position, each member casts a vote for whomever they think is worthy of the job. Those who receive at least two votes are then brought up to the front of the room. The same number of Bibles or hymn books as the number of candidates are then placed on a table; inside one of these books is a piece of paper with a Scripture verse. Whoever chooses this book becomes the new church leader. In selecting a minister or deacon in this manner, the Amish believe he is chosen by God. The bishops are also chosen by lot from the available and worthy deacons and ministers.

A church official is chosen for life, a cause for joy as well as sorrow to the family because of the great burden of responsibility it entails. Church leaders maintain their previous jobs; they do not receive a salary, since in the eyes of God none in the community is better or worse than any other.

A TYPICAL CHURCH SERVICE

Church is held every other week at one of the member's houses. (During the off weeks, the Amish are encouraged to visit other churches, keeping the ties of community strong between the many groups.) Amish houses are large, usually with moving partitions on the first floor to open up the house to accommodate a gathering. Holding church in the home reinforces the Amish belief that a true fellowship of Christ doesn't need a separate building in which to worship.

This practice is part of the mortar which binds the Amish; their strong sense of family and togetherness seals their practice of following God's way at home, at church, and at play. It also gives all the members of the church at least one chance every year to visit in the homes of other members, and to see if anyone is becoming too worldly in their home furnishings. In contrast, the Old Order Mennonites, who are very similar in appearance and beliefs, worship in a meeting house.

Church usually begins around 9:00 AM with the members filing into the house in an orderly fashion, the oldest first and the youngest and the unmarried last. Women and men sit separately on backless benches, a practice that instills and reinforces personal discipline. As the first hymn is announced and the singing commences, the men remove their hats and the church leaders retire to the *abroth*, or council, to discuss matters of importance and to decide who will give the two morning sermons.

Left:
Before church service and later while waiting to share the Sunday meal, young boys play in the barnyard. The young, single people are the last to be seated for both the service and the meal.

The second hymn is always the traditional Hymn of Praise, *Das Lob Sang*. The singing stops when the leaders return and the service continues with the first minister "making the beginning," preaching the first sermon. This thirty-minute sermon is followed by kneeling in silent prayer, then a Scripture reading from the New Testament.

The second sermon, given by either the bishop or another minister, follows and lasts about an hour and a half. During this time the children, who are usually sitting in the back, are given a small snack to help them make it until the meal. After the main sermon any minister or deacon present may give a testimonial, then the congregation kneels again while a prayer is read from the *Christenpflicht*. At the conclusion of the prayer, everyone is seated while the deacon makes church announcements (including where the next meeting will be held), "publishes" any marriages, and then, if there is to be a church meeting, excuses non-members. The formal service always ends with a hymn.

When church ends and the house is emptied, the benches are removed and tables are set for the communal meal. The same menu is served every week so that there is no competition among those who make and serve the food. The meal is simple, consisting of breads, pickles, jams, jellies, and butter, sandwiches or soup, and pies. The seating order is the same as that for church, with men and women sitting at separate tables. The bishop and the ministers always eat first, in company with the older, married men and women.

When everyone is seated, the bishop signals to those present and a silent prayer is said; at the meal's end, another silent prayer of thanksgiving is offered. The tables are then reset without washing the dishes (they are merely wiped clean), and the next set of people is fed, with the same prayer rituals observed. This continues until all have eaten, a process that may last until mid-afternoon. Visiting is a big part of Amish socialization and fellowship, and members either stay at the host's farm or call on others throughout the afternoon.

Left:
The family farm is the center of Amish life. Births, weddings, church services, and funerals all occur at home.

Above:
To accommodate many vehicles during a church service, horses are put out to pasture or tied in the stables while buggies are lined up in the driveway or lane. Within a particular church, all of the buggies are the same according to the *Ordnung*.

Right:
The *Ordnung* dictates austerity of dress both for work and for church. Since everyone wears the same style and color of clothing, there is no competition for being the best-dressed member of the community. Men and boys dress similarly.

BELIEFS AND PRACTICES

The foundation of the Anabaptists' faith exists in their belief that the church should be a body of voluntary adult members, sanctioned by adult baptism. Joining the church requires a total dedication and adherence to all of the church doctrines and a sacrifice of individuality for the benefit of the group. This commitment is not taken lightly, and once entered into, any deviance from it could result in the errant person's excommunication from the brotherhood.

Baptism usually takes place between the ages of sixteen and twenty-one, with women typically being baptized at an earlier age. When a young person decides that he or she is ready to join the church, they inform the bishop; a group of youths usually joins at the same time. For the five or six church services preceding the day of baptism, the young people are given confirmation classes by the elders in the *abroth*, with the bishop as their primary teacher. Before they are received into the church, usually on the day of the baptism, they are offered one last chance to back out of the commitment.

After the second sermon, the congregation is asked to stand while the recipients kneel during prayer. The candidates are asked three questions affirming their faith before the bishop cups his hands above the head of each youth, beginning with the boys. As the deacon pours water through his hands three times, the bishop blesses the person in the name of the Father, and the Son, and the Holy Ghost. The bishop then offers his hand to each boy in turn, helps him rise, greets him with the "holy kiss" (a common greeting between members of the church), and bids him go in peace. The girls are greeted in the same manner by either the bishop's or the deacon's wife.

Communion, the affirmation of one's total faith, is held in the spring and the fall of each year. In the course of the

Below:
A Nebraska Amishman's appearance is much plainer than that of some other sects. His hair is worn longer (collar length), his hat brim is wider, and his clothing is patterned after the old colonial style.

Left:
The Amish consider themselves stewards of the land. Often Amish farms have beautiful flower gardens surrounding their yards. Adornments inside the house are frowned upon, but beauty provided by nature is considered part of God's handiwork.

Following page:
Both Amish and Mennonites are very religious. Frequently, Mennonite farmers put signs quoting Biblical Scripture in their fields adjoining roads. In the background is an Amish one-room schoolhouse.

FOR WHOSOEVER SHALL
CALL UPON THE
NAME OF THE LORD
SHALL BE SAVED. ROM.10:13

preceding church service, a members' meeting is held during which the bishop recounts any news from the biannual church leaders' gathering. If there are any proposed changes in practices, the congregation votes to confirm or reject them. The bishop also brings up any disputes between members and tries to resolve these issues. If the entire church body is not at peace, communion will be postponed until the time when church unity resumes; in some cases, this type of rift has lasted several years.

The communion service is nearly the same as the weekly one, differing only in that it lasts well into the afternoon. During the normal lunch time, a small snack is set up in an adjoining room and members take turns leaving the service to eat. The main sermon, lasting up to three hours, is usually timed to end close to 3:00 PM, the supposed time when Jesus Christ died on the cross. After his sermon, the bishop blesses the bread and the grape wine and each in turn is passed out to the members. As each person partakes, he is reminded that these are the symbols of Christ's body and blood.

After communion, the deacons prepare buckets of water and as the last hymn is sung, the rite of foot washing begins. The men and women pair off (in same-sex couples) and wash each other's feet, symbolizing Christ's servanthood. This act of humility is accentuated by the washer stooping instead of kneeling during the washing, and is ended with a holy kiss and blessing between the pair.

At the end of the service, each family gives the deacon an offering in the amount of their choice, put toward the alms fund. This fund is used to aid the poor of the congregation as well as anyone experiencing short-term difficulties, such as recently bereaved widows. Unless the fund runs dry, this is the only time during the year that members are asked to contribute a monetary gift.

Left:
Children ride in the rear of buggies behind their parents. When the weather is warm enough, a cloth flap is rolled up at the back, allowing the children to look out as the family travels.

Above:
Church is held every other Sunday at one of the member's houses. Between twenty and thirty-five families comprise a church. The first floor of an Amish house has removable partitions in order to make room for everyone.

Throughout the tales of the *Martyr's Mirror*, nonresistance and love of thy neighbor are stressed. Early in life, the Amish are taught never to raise arms against another human being. In the past, this practice of pacifism resulted in their persecution in Europe as well as some ravaging attacks by native Americans in the New World.

One well-known story involves Jacob Hochstetler, Jr., from Berks County, Pennsylvania. As the story goes, his family was attacked by a group of Indians one night. Jacob's sons took up guns to fight the Indians, but he made them put the guns away, resulting in the massacre of most of his family and the capture of Jacob and two of his sons. They were separated and taken to western Pennsylvania, but after several years of captivity they were eventually reunited. Some Amish did serve in the military, particularly during the Civil War, but the majority avoided it.

The Amish are not the only conscientious objectors in today's society; many of the "Peace Churches," the Mennonites and the Church of the Brethren, share this belief. As the government demanded service from the young men of this country, alternative service was devised. During World War II, many conscientious objectors served in health- and service-related fields, as medics, litter bearers, or office workers; still more were relieved from military service with farm deferments.

SEPARATION OF CHURCH AND STATE

The persecution of Anabaptists during their early years drove home the belief that government could not be trusted. Throughout their history, the Amish have contended with different governments trying to control certain aspects of their beliefs and lives, including school attendance, military service, the paying of social security taxes, and the wearing of hardhats on non-Amish construction jobs. The complete separation of church and state is something the Amish believe

Above:
An Amish farm at sunrise is an especially peaceful sight, but even at this early hour, the family is starting the daily chores. The cows need to be milked, the eggs gathered, and the other farm animals fed.

Left:
The exterior of the Amish house is very plain. Most are painted white, no shutters are attached, and only pull-down shades are used at the windows. In contrast, the Nebraska Amish strip their homes of all paint to expose the underlying wood and use plain brown butcher's paper as window coverings.

wholly in and, if necessary, they are willing to go to jail for their beliefs.

The Amish weren't always so staunchly against government. There are many records from the late 1700s and throughout the 1800s showing Amish citizens holding public offices such as school directors, tax collectors, and township commissioners. Even though they don't hold public offices today, the Amish will on occasion vote in local elections on issues directly related to their own interests (such as the proposal of highways cutting through the heart of their farmlands).

And despite what most people think, the Amish pay the same taxes as the rest of society. The only tax from which they are exempt is social security, with one exception: an Amish person working for a non-Amish employer must pay into social security even though the benefits to that worker are rarely collected. With the support of extended families and the care given to the elderly by the community, the Amish forego government aid; only on rare occasions do they accept any type of social security or welfare payments.

Above:
When families live near each other, they may all go to church together. Here, several families travel in an open carriage.

Right:
The Church of the Brethren shares a common Anabaptist ancestry with the Amish. This man is celebrating the one-hundredth anniversary of his home church by dressing in the garb of a century ago. Similarities can be seen between the Brethren of old and the Amish of today.

CHAPTER 2

SACRIFICE AND FAITH: THE HOME AND THE FARM

The adage "Faith in works" expresses the daily credo of the Amish. It probably has its origin in Scripture: Matthew 7:20 states, "By their fruits ye shall know them." When asked, Amishmen will explain that one can't have faith without substance, without every aspect of the daily routine mirroring one's deep faith and trust in God.

Living by their word and devoting their entire existence to worshipping God is the sole way for the Amish to attain salvation. Only through constant faith and devotion to the Scriptures, avoidance of worldly temptations, support from church and community, and the strong bond of family do the brethren find the confidence to let their actions speak for themselves.

THE HOME

Amish life centers around the home. Church services, marriages, funerals, births, virtually every important event in the life of an Amishman occurs here. The kitchen is the focal point, where the family meets for meals and for fellowship in the evenings. Since most homes don't have central heating, the busy kitchen is the most logical place for them to gather as they cook, sew, read, or share in the day's activities and any important news.

The house itself is unpretentious with simple, yet functional, furnishings and no pictures. There are no curtains, either; pull-down shades are used at the windows (in the case of the Nebraska Amish, plain brown butcher's paper is used as a window covering). If mirrors are found at all, there are only small ones present; this absence originates in the Bible, with God commanding his people to make no graven images unto themselves. The Amish view the mirror as a sign of pride, as they do any gaudy decorations in and around the home.

The exterior of the house is usually a plain white, but some churches allow the painting of a gate green or the sills around the doors and windows sky blue. Some Nebraska Amish buy homes

Left:
An Amishman works from dawn until dusk. To the Amish, hard work is good for the soul. The discipline and sacrifice involved in running a farm without modern tractors and machinery helps them stay close to nature and to God.

from the "English"—a term used by the Amish to describe anyone non-Amish—and immediately strip these houses of all paint or siding, leaving just the raw wood exposed. Although their homes are plain, their gardens are often exquisite, reflecting their love of the land and their sense of God-given stewardship.

A significant difference between so-called English and Amish households exists in the allowance of electricity and telephones within the house or on the farm. Most Amish do not use electricity, resorting to kerosene or gas lamps for light, and most do not have phones on their property. The strictness of each sect's *Ordnung* dictates to what extent bottled natural gas, gasoline, or diesel fuel are used. Even among the Old Order sects, there is tremendous variety. Inside, the home runs the gamut from stoves run by coal, wood, or gas to chill springhouses or kerosene- or gas-run refrigerators for

food storage and hand-rung or gas-powered washing machines. The Amish do not oppose battery power, so they may own a battery-operated shaver or a calculator.

Outdoor practices vary as well. Grass may be mowed with a push mower, while the weeds may be cut with a gasoline-powered weed-eater. On one farm all plows and field tools may be simple, while on another farm gasoline- or diesel-run machinery can be prevalent. Water is obtained in a variety of ways: hand pumps, windmills, gravity-fed springs, waterwheels, water rams, and gasoline or diesel pumps inside wells are all used.

To avoid any temptation to gossip and to maintain the family's separation from the outside world, telephones are not permitted within the house itself. However, the Amish do use them. In some areas a community phone, owned and maintained by several families, is located at the end of a farm lane.

Above:
Hex signs were used as protection against evil spells. These colorful markers can still be found adorning the barns of many of the Pennsylvania Dutch. These people more closely resemble the Mennonites in their habits, using electricity, cars, and most modern amenities.

Right:
Many Pennsylvania Dutch barns are ornately decorated. Besides hex signs on the sides, they also have carved door frames.

Left:
Sunset offers relief from daily chores. Without electricity, homes are lit either by kerosene or gas lanterns. The old saying, "You go to bed with the chickens and rise with the roosters," applies to the Amish way of life.

As a community service, a local phone company may place a public phone at a crossroads within a short distance of many families. Some Amish may rent a phone in the shed, barn, or basement of a non-Amish family, just as they may place a food freezer in these homes. Out of necessity or pure practicality, Amish businessmen usually have phones located in a nearby shed or right outside of their business.

Telephone use and its subsequent shunning caused a major rift inside the Old Order Amish community in the first part of this century; the resulting splinter group, now called the Beachy Amish, favored the use of the telephone, as well as electricity, within the home. Today, this group has become a large, viable sect with congregations throughout North and Central America and as far away as Paraguay.

THE FARM

Farming is vital to Amish life. Since they consider themselves stewards of God's creation, any desecration of land would be a sacrilege. They are considered to be among the world's best farmers, as their use of crop rotation and natural fertilizers such as manure has transformed barren land into fertile breadbaskets. It is very rare for an Amishman to sell his land to a non-Amish person, unless an entire group moves *en masse* out of an area.

Traditionally, the farm is passed from one generation to the next, reinforcing the importance of keeping its soil fertile and rich. With land at a premium in most areas, turning the farm

over to the next generation while they are still young is an ideal situation for all involved. Still, the growing Amish population, coupled with the rising cost of good farmland and the loss of land due to urban expansion, has caused many young Amish farmers to travel the United States in search of cheaper land.

The typical Amish farm is between sixty and one hundred acres except in the Midwest, where crop yield is lower per acre and the farms correspondingly larger. Farms are small enough to be family-run but large enough to produce ample quantities of food for the family and provide some surplus to sell. Alfalfa, corn, wheat, tobacco, and potatoes are typical crops; sometimes a small orchard is added. Most farms have dairy cows whose milk is either sent for commercial production or used to make cheese.

Some compromises are made on the farm; what is stated by the *Ordnung* and what is followed may differ markedly. For example, tractors are forbidden for field work though some can be found in the barnyard, and where rubber tires are prohibited, farm machinery is fitted with steel wheels. Because of state agricultural regulations, some churches have ratified the use of stainless steel milk-storage tanks, cooled and agitated by diesel motors.

In some sects, belt-driven machinery helps fill silos, and large pieces of equipment such as hay balers are run by gasoline; still other sects only allow the use of non-mechanized, horse-drawn plows and harrows. A good horse is very

Left:
Belgian draft and Clydesdale horses, as well as mules, are used on the farm to pull heavy equipment. Depending on the task, as many as six horses are hitched to the machinery. Usually, only one person controls the team.

Following page:
Everyone helps with the farm chores. During the harvest, entire families will gather in the fields to help cut the corn, wheat, and tobacco. It takes many hands to bundle sheaves of wheat together so they can dry in the sun. The dried stalks are used for straw.

Left:
Corn is one of the main crops grown by the Amish. Field corn is grown to feed the livestock throughout the winter months. At harvest time, several farmers may gather to help one another with the daunting task of the corn harvest.

Left:
A typical Amish farm covers between sixty and one hundred acres. Land is passed down from one generation to the next. With both the increase in urban development and the greater number of Amish children surviving to adulthood, farmland has become scarce in many areas.

Left:
Lancaster County, Pennsylvania, contains some of the richest farmland in the state. Most of the land is owned by the Amish. Their practice of rotating crops and using natural fertilizers has earned the county the nickname, "The Garden Spot of Pennsylvania."

Left:
With the countryside blanketed in snow, the Amish farm becomes a winter wonderland. When snows are deep, the Amish enlist the help of "English" neighbors to help plow out their lanes.

important to the Amish, although there is no standard work horse; powerfully built Belgian draft and Clydesdale horses and the dependable mule are the favorites. The buying and selling of these animals, either privately or at auctions, is a frequent activity.

THE ROLES AND OCCUPATIONS OF MEN

Farmwork is all-consuming, and every member of the family helps during the spring planting and fall harvest seasons. Still, it is the primary responsibility of men to keep the farm productive and successful even through years of natural hardships and disasters. This responsibility applies to church leaders, too, even though their church responsibilities take precedence over their own farm work; consequently, they sometimes hire help for the farm. Leaving the harder work of the farm to his son and grandsons, the "retired" farmer does not grow idle. Most older men take up another profession—such as making wood crafts or repairing things—to "grow old with."

Sometimes farmland is not available; on a small farm, the youngest sons may face the choice of moving out of the area or seeking a different trade. Most men who have to find other occupations enter fields useful to the Amish community. Buggy making or repair, leather work (such as fashioning harnesses), blacksmithing, and cabinetry are popular trades, while clock making and furniture design have achieved the status of an art form among some meticulous Amish craftsmen.

Some men have had to find work outside of the community as carpenters with construction firms. (Although rare, some women work outside of the home in restaurants and shops as well.) Becoming a "lunch-box society" poses a threat to Amish segregation from the outside world, and it is this fear that keeps many close to home and farm.

In times of need, the Amish sense of community shines. Should a neighbor's barn be lost to fire or storm the men will gather together for a barn raising, sometimes replacing the structure in a single day. This solidarity is not always limited to their fellow Amish; some men will also volunteer to help clean up and rebuild the structures of their "English" neighbors.

Right:
Raising ostriches for food and leather goods has become very popular across the United States. Some Amish farmers as well have taken up this profitable venture.

Above:
Even though all farm equipment is pulled by horse or mule, some pieces are run by
gasoline motors. An Amish farmer may have a gasoline-powered thrasher or a hay baler.

Right:
Mowing and gathering hay is a task which involves the whole family. Some Amish do the entire chore by hand, from loading the wagons in the field to unloading the hay into the lofts.

Right:
Many Amish farmers now use gasoline-operated hay balers in the fields. One person drives the team of horses which pulls the baler and wagon; another takes the bales as they come off the conveyor belt and stacks them by hand on the wagon.

Right:
All field work on an Amish farm is done with horse-drawn equipment. Some churches, however, allow tractors to be used in the barnyard to operate belt-driven equipment for filling the silos.

THE ROLES OF WOMEN AND CHILDREN

Although the Amish have a patriarchal society, women still play a very important role. Prohibited from leading a church, a woman can still nominate and vote for candidates for leadership in the church. She is a co-owner of the family farm, writing checks and purchasing items at market and public auctions, and she is certainly an equal partner in life, garnering respect from her husband for her pivotal role.

While both parents are involved with child rearing, it is the woman's chief responsibility. The Amish woman is mistress of the household, responsible for its upkeep both inside and out, and for all food preparations, both daily and long-term. She makes and mends the clothes, and plants, cares for, and harvests the flower and vegetable gardens. Though humility is honored and individuality is dampened, a woman can shine in her skills as a gardener, a baker, or as a quilt designer. Work is hard, both in the home and on the farm, but it is welcomed by the Amish and they embrace it with vigor.

With its presence at church services, funerals, weddings, barn raisings and "frolics," food—one of the main responsibilities of the Amish woman—is obviously an integral part of Amish life. To the Amish, the way to a healthy and happy body is through devotion, hard work, and good, nutritional food. Meals are a time of fellowship and plenty; their rigorous work schedules insure hearty appetites all around.

Increased use of refrigerators and freezers has made it easier to keep food for longer periods of time, but the preserving of fruits, vegetables, and meats is still an eagerly-awaited activity during the summer and fall. Most meats are smoked, cured, dried, or canned; ham is a favorite. The Amish women are renowned for their baked goods, and specialty items such

Above:
Girls of all ages help in food preparation. At an early age, their chores may be snapping green beans or picking vegetables from the garden. With large families, feeding everyone is a full-time occupation.

Left:
Without electricity to provide refrigeration or freezing, much food is canned for long-time storage. At the end of the harvest, shelves are stocked full. By the following spring, most of the food is gone.

as shoe-fly pie (a molasses- and brown sugar-based desert), fruit pies, and sticky buns, as well as apple butter, chow-chow, and pot pie lure many tourists to the Amish country.

Children are considered blessings of God. They are loved and tended not only by the parents, but also by grandparents and the extended family. The Amish child grows up feeling wanted and cared for, with a sense of stability and belonging to an ageless tradition. Children begin to do chores when they are quite young, sometimes as early as six years old; at this age, they may help snap green beans or wash the dishes. It is happy work, as they enjoy the company of their brothers, sisters, and cousins. Despite a heavy work load (apportioned according to age), they still manage to play with board games and toys like tops or wagons, and participate in group activities such as "fox and geese" and corner ball.

Introduced as babies to the discipline and strictness of the church, Amish children are brought up learning respect and manners. Although a spanking is given if warranted, silence acts as the deterrent for most misbehavior. Even among sometimes curious and rebellious adolescents, the strong, comforting ties of both family and church usually bring a roving youth back into the fold.

Above:
Women are an important part of life on the farm and in the home. Their opinions are valued in all decisions; they run the household, pay the bills, and purchase items needed by the family.

Left:
Even the smallest Amish child has a job to do while working in the fields. Since children are a blessing from God, making them feel as if they are a vital part of the family is very important. Sometimes, of course, they take time off to play a game of tag around the field.

CLOTHING AND HAIR STYLES

To the casual observer, what most clearly distinguishes the Amish from the modern world is their appearance. Although the Amish all seem to be uniform in their dress, there are subtle differences between the sects which signify their degree of simplicity and modesty. However, there is no sense of pride or competitiveness among those within a single order, all of whom wear the same styles of clothing and hair.

Men usually wear jackets without lapels, broadfall pants (a type of trouser with a large flap of cloth closed by buttons instead of a zipper), suspenders, and broad-brimmed hats (straw during the summer and black for dress and winter). Black pants and coats with white shirts are worn on Sundays and other special occasions; everyday clothing generally consists of dark-colored pants and solid-colored shirts. For some Amishmen, a colorful exception occurs in hunting seasons: to comply with state game laws, the Amish hunter wears a bright, fluorescent orange vest and hat.

The Amish beard is distinctive, worn without a mustache, a practice adopted in order to distinguish brethren from soldiers during the time of the European persecutions. In most cases, men grow their beards after marriage and they are never trimmed. Their hair, however, is kept at a consistent length, cropped at the ear. In contrast, a Nebraska Amishman wears his hair longer (usually collar length), his hat brim broader, and, always, a white, more colonial-style shirt and brown pants without suspenders.

The women dress in plain colors—no prints, plaids, lace, or frills. Black is usually worn for religious services, and subdued colors are worn for everyday activities. Both women and girls wear aprons of white, black, or a color matching their dresses. Most don a cape, a triangular piece of cloth worn by tucking one corner in at the waist in back, draping the rest over the shoulders, crossing the ends in front, and fastening them to the apron with straight pins. (Typically, Amish clothing is secured with straight pins, snaps, or hooks and eyes.)

Above:
Clothes are hung outside to dry in the wind and sun. Even in the dead of winter, a passerby can see laundry hanging from the lines of an Amish household.

Right:
Amish men wear straw hats for farmwork and on other occasions during the summer months. Straw hats have become a favorite of many people, including non-Amish farmers. They are not only cool but also offer protection from the sun.

Right:
The clothing of Old Order Brethren is similar to that of the Amish. A woman has a *kapp* for her head and wears a plain, print dress which is covered in front by a cape that reaches across the shoulders to the back where it is fastened at the waist by straight pins.

Instead of cutting their hair, Amish women wear it long, parted in the middle and pulled back into a severe bun at the base of the neck. As dictated by I Corinthians 11, women always cover their heads. Their prayer covering, or *kapp*, varies in size, shape, and material depending on the sect. Over this, they may wear a black bonnet for certain occasions or a simple sunbonnet while working in the garden.

Footwear for the Amish is simple but functional; if not barefoot, men and boys wear work boots for the farm and plain black shoes for church. The women wear plain, black lace-up shoes for most occasions. Sneakers for both sexes are becoming more common, with style and color varying according to age. No jewelry is worn by either sex, including wedding rings.

Above:
Modern appliances are not found in the Amish household. Clothes are washed by hand and put through a hand ringer to squeeze out the water. Although some Amish use gas-powered washing machines, it is usually the exception.

Following page:
Amish women visit while attending a public auction. Notice the uniformity in dress with the black head coverings, black coats, and subdued colors of their everyday dress.

TRANSPORTATION

While technology and travel have driven many modern families apart by hundreds of miles, the Amish's central core of family, church, and community has persevered, offering a support group that's only a few miles away whenever it is needed.

There is no better symbol of the Amish people's separation from mainstream America than the horse and buggy. The Amish believe that traveling by horse is another display of sacrifice, keeping their lives at a pace that is more in line with God and nature; by not conforming to a more mobile and faster society, they have embraced a simpler, more disciplined way of life. Being limited by the distance a buggy can travel in one day also helps maintain their close-knit community.

There are over one hundred different styles of horse-drawn buggies and carriages. These include open buggies, buck-board wagons, and closed carriages which vary in their extent of enclosure and in their colored tops, ranging from yellow and white to gray and black. The local *Ordnung* dictates if buggies may have windshields, wipers, chrome fittings, rear-view mirrors, or turn signals.

Civil law also plays a part in Pennsylvania; for example, buggies must have both flashing lights and large, fluorescent orange triangles on the rear to increase visibility at night. Lights vary by sect; some use battery-operated lamps while others, like the Nebraska Amish, use kerosene lamps with reflectors as running lights.

Below:
Along roadsides throughout the Amish countryside, signs like this warn drivers to be on the lookout for Amish buggies. Each year, fatalities occur as a result of motorists driving too fast for conditions along the back roads the Amish buggies frequent.

Left:
Holmes County, Ohio, boasts the largest population of Amish in the United States. Styles of buggies and manner of dress distinguishes these sects from others around the country.

Right:
Young, unmarried Amish couples usually travel in a "courting buggy." These buggies are open with no roof. On warm weekend nights during the summer and early fall, many courting buggies may be seen on local roads as young people go to different farms for singings and "frolics."

Left:
There are over one hundred different styles of horse-drawn buggies and carriages. Several different types may be used by the same sect. A family may own a formal buggy, a buckboard wagon for hauling items, and a small carriage or buggy to use when visiting friends.

Below:
In Pennsylvania, state law dictates the use of large, fluorescent triangles on all buggies and wagons traveling public roads.

Although the Amish don't own cars they are permitted to ride in them, usually paying the non-Amish owner a fare. Amish people will also use public transportation such as trains and buses, but they are forbidden by the *Ordnung* to travel by plane. Bicycles, too, are proscribed because they have inflatable rubber tires, but in some congregations roller skates and scooters with hard rubber tires are permitted.

The increased use of automobiles, electricity, and telephones in this century became key factors in the many divisions among the Amish and Mennonites. The New Order Amish may still use horses and buggies, but they also have electricity and phones in their houses and use tractors on their farms. The Beachy Amish dress plainly but use cars, electricity, and phones and, perhaps not coincidentally, are also deeply involved in world missionary work. The Hutterites, like the Beachy Amish, are more worldly, but they differ in that they are a communal society, jointly owning the land on which they live, sharing residences, and eating together as a group.

In appearance and tradition, there is not much difference between the Old Order Amish, Old Order Mennonites, and Old Order River Brethren; and though they share the religious beliefs and practices of the Old Orders, many of the groups comprising the Church of the Brethren and the Mennonites have assimilated into today's society, adopting the dress and lifestyle of modern America.

Left:
Some Amish sects use battery-operated running lights on their buggies at night. A few states have also mandated that buggies be equipped with red flashing lights.

Right:
Horses are a favorite means of transportation among the youth. When children are too young to drive a buggy alone, they use a horse, scooter, or even skates to travel places.

CHAPTER 3
CELEBRATIONS
AND
RITES OF PASSAGE

In Merle Good's book *Who Are the Amish?*, the seasons of Amish life are likened to the rhythms of nature; they live close to the earth and are both dependent upon and susceptible to nature's whims. If one views Amish life as movements in nature's symphony, the comparison becomes more obvious.

Springtime, of course, represents the beginning of life. For the Amish, it is a time of planting crops and starting gardens, just as the earth is again green with young plants pushing up from the soil. It is also the season for newlyweds to start their own households. For children, the springtime of their lives is exciting but never carefree, full of games and learning in school, at home, and at social gatherings.

The summer season is the busiest in Amish life. Full of hard work in the home and on the farm, it is a time of family growth and togetherness. The warmth of summer stirs everyone to visit, take buggy rides or walks, participate in ball games, and work "frolics." Some crops mature while others are planted, farmers' markets overflow with the surplus of the many vegetable gardens, and young people start thinking about their futures as courtship rituals begin.

Autumn is harvest season—a time of plenty. It is the time to reap the bounties of the land and to say prayers of thanksgiving for what God has given. It is also a time to replenish the earth and prepare the soil for next year's crops. In the autumn of life, the older Amish "retire" to make way for the younger generation, all the while remaining vital in the community of man and God.

Winter is a quiet time around the farm, a time to reflect, rest, repair, and create. Even in this relative stillness, a new cycle of activity begins. Early winter is the season for weddings, when two lives join together to start a new verse, a new cycle of celebration, a continued walk through God's garden.

Right:
In Lancaster County, Pennsylvania, there are
many covered bridges throughout the countryside.
Watching a horse and buggy travel across one of these
recalls the days when life was simpler and slower.

COURTSHIP

The Amish maintain their close-knit communities by actively knowing and relating to one another, with their home-based church meetings, barn raisings, and frequent visits to each others' homes. Living in close proximity certainly helps; having the support of family and friends during times of joy and sorrow, sickness and strife, creates a sense of togetherness, a feeling of belonging to a larger group that will never fail you.

Since almost all socializing is done within the district, by the time young people are ready for courtship they have known the person of their fancy for many years. Unlike dating in the modern world, it is never publicly announced that a certain boy likes a certain girl. Courtship takes place covertly—a courting couple will not be seen riding or walking together during the day but only at night, under the cover of darkness.

There are plenty of opportunities for young, unmarried people to interact. "Singings" are one of their favorite types of get-togethers. Usually held on Sunday evenings at the same house as the church service, singings are a time of fun, fellowship, and music. Singing the faster and livelier hymns from the *Ausband*, the youth combine enjoyment with worship. Since no musical instruments are played and there is no written music, the songs are sung from memory.

At singings, young men who are interested in becoming singers (leaders) during regular church services can practice, as older men, who have sung the tunes for years, help them with the melodies. Girls are allowed to choose the hymns to sing, although they usually don't lead them. At the end of the evening, couples pair off for the ride home; this private time in the buggy gives the two a chance to get to know one another.

There are other times during the year when young people may socialize in a legitimate manner. Sometimes a farmer will organize a "corn husking," where young people gather at the host's house to husk corn. Boys and girls are paired off in the field, either by their own choosing or with the help of the farmer. Laughing and talking prevails as the boy tears down the stalks and the two share husking duties, continuing until supper is announced. Entering the house in pairs, the young people are fed by the host family. Afterward, a typical husking party moves to the barn where games are played until the early hours.

As two young people become more interested in each other, courtship becomes more secretive and fervent. The boy will begin to visit the girl at her home after everyone has gone to bed, visiting for hours in the quiet of the kitchen as they learn more about each other. In the past "bundling" was a common practice. The couple retired to one of the bedrooms (usually the girl's), wrapped themselves in quilts, and continued their

Left:
Amish youth oftentimes drive their own buggies to church. Afterwards, they may travel to another farm for a softball game or a singing later in the evening. A singing is attended mainly by unmarried boys and girls and is used as an organized and chaperoned mixer.

private conversation. The quilts weren't so much to prevent any misconduct as to keep the two warm, since houses then, as now, lacked central heating. Sometimes a board was placed between them to make the separation more complete, but even then some girls ended up getting pregnant.

Keeping their relationship secret is very important to the young couple; if things don't work out, no one will be the wiser. When the couple is certain they want to get married (most often when they are between twenty and twenty-three) the man pays his favorite minister a secret visit, usually just before bedtime. Explaining his intentions, he asks the minister to go to the woman's home to approach her parents with his offer. The minister visits the woman's home, again before bedtime and maintaining secrecy, and presents the parents with the proposal. He then returns to the man with the parents' reply and, if it is favorable, the man gives the minister a wedding date and asks him to make the arrangements for the public announcement.

At the church service prior to the wedding day, the deacon "publishes" the engagement and announces the wedding date. Up until this time, the only people who are privy to the impending wedding are the future bride and groom, the bride's parents, and the minister and deacon.

WEDDINGS

Although not necessary for courtship, church membership is required for marriage. Weddings are performed on Tuesdays or Thursdays, usually during November, December, or January. The bride wears either an all-white garment or a white apron and cape over her dress (white is worn as a symbol of virginity); the groom is dressed in his Sunday best, black coat and trousers. The bridal party includes four atten-

dants, two girls and two boys. Usually held in the home of the bride, the wedding may be attended by several hundred people; the wedding day feasts and festivities are always held at the bride's house.

The four-hour service begins around 9:00 AM and follows the general pattern of a Sunday service. During the opening hymns the bride and groom accompany the bishop and ministers to the *abroth* for last-minute counseling and advice. Since divorce is unthinkable and punished by immediate excommunication, marriage is not entered into lightly. The hymns, sermon, and scriptures are standardized for most weddings, and stress the roles of the man and woman and the importance of obedience, love, and family. At the end of the main sermon, the couple exchanges vows similar to those taken in other Protestant weddings. The service concludes with testimony from other ministers present, the benediction, a prayer, and a hymn. The remainder of the day is full of food, fellowship, and celebration.

During the feast, the bride and the groom sit at a special corner table in the main room and are served first. The rest of the guests are served in shifts, with toasts and songs scattered throughout the meal. During the afternoon the young people exit to the barn, where there are games and dancing; the newlyweds join in for the last time. Singing, eating, dancing, and visiting will continue until late in the night.

Like all young couples, the newlyweds receive many useful gifts including tinware, quilts, bedding, and dishes. Throughout the next several months, the new couple travels and stays at the homes of parents, siblings, aunts, uncles, and cousins. In the spring, both sets of parents will help the two set up their new home, offering such gifts as horses, cows, plows, and furniture.

Right:
Amish men don't grow beards until after they marry. After the wedding, they are expected to have a beard before the next communion, which usually occurs the following spring.

Left:
An Amish family sometimes walks to church or to a meeting instead of driving their buggy. Small children are either carried or pulled behind the parents in a wagon. Wagons can be used because they have solid rubber tires, not inflatable ones.

Left:
Fathers take an active role in child rearing. Working in the fields, fathers teach their young boys to till the soil, rotate crops, and plow to produce abundant crops. Sometimes, fathers have to comfort their children when things go wrong.

Left:
It takes many hands to help with the oat harvest. Using pitchforks, the men and boys load and unload the wagon by hand. This type of work frolic is enjoyed by all, with the host family feeding all the workers a hardy meal during the day.

Left:
Families prefer to walk to church if meetings are held close enough to their homes. The shortest route to the neighbor's farm may be across a field or down the railroad track.

Following page:
At an early age, Amish boys learn to repair farm equipment and tend livestock. By the age of twelve, many boys can harness a team of horses and direct them in the fields. They also become adept at running the barnyard chores.

BIRTH AND THE ROLES OF MODERN MEDICINE

As children are treasured and large families are considered a blessing, young Amish couples waste no time in beginning their new families. Most children are born at home with a midwife in attendance. In some communities, there are birthing houses where expectant women stay as the time of their delivery nears. Today it is not uncommon for women to visit a medical doctor during pregnancy, although there are usually no doctors present during birth.

Because of the close relations in some communities it's not uncommon for cousins to marry each other, and gene pools can be very limited. There are several recorded cases of both fatal and non-fatal genetic disorders; in one Lancaster County, Pennsylvania, community, for example, the condition of hexadactylism, or having six fingers, is common. Ironically, with the advances of modern medicine Amish infant and child mortality has decreased, compounding the problem of a rising population with insufficient land for everyone.

The Amish are not opposed to formal medical or dental care. They prefer to treat their ailments with home remedies but will resort to professional medical help in emergencies, including hospitalization for serious illnesses. They are rarely vaccinated for the common childhood diseases, but when epidemics occur—such as polio and measles have in the past several decades—the Amish will permit doctors to vaccinate anyone at risk.

Above:
Young Amish children aren't put into childcare centers during the day. Instead, they travel with their mother wherever she goes, learning important tasks by watching her. The strengths of the Amish family, both in emotional and physical support, are instilled early.

Left:
Amish children are exact copies of their parents in appearance and dress. Amish families don't practice birth control and families are usually large, but many hands are needed to help with work both on the farm and in the home.

HOLIDAYS

Even though the Amish work very hard most of the year, their calendar does contain several holidays. They do not observe national holidays or the birthdays of heroes, since this would demonstrate nationalism and an acceptance of government. Many of their holidays coincide with religious observances; they are days of relative leisure, oftentimes worship, and are always filled with the joy of visiting.

As with all Christians, Easter is an important religious holiday; the Amish also observe Good Friday, Easter Monday, and Ascension Day. Having religious undertones, Thanksgiving and Christmas are included as holidays, as is New Year's Day. Unlike many non-Amish people, the Amish observe a traditional Christmas, celebrating its true meaning and escaping the overpowering trappings of modern glitz and commercialism.

Above:
Even during the busy harvest season, children find time to play. Baseball is a favorite activity
of both boys and girls. In some communities, bicycles are permitted but only if they have hard
rubber tires. Any object with inflatable rubber tires is prohibited according to the *Ordnung*.

Above:
Children of all ages enjoy scooters.
Used mostly as a means of transportation,
younger children ride them to school.

FUNERALS

Death is an accepted fact within the Amish way of life. Following the principle, "What God hath giveth, God will taketh away," they treat death not only as a time of sorrow and loss, but as a time of support and giving as well. A death in their community brings the Amish together in their loss. Family and friends take care of the funeral arrangements and perform all of the farm and household chores. If finances are a problem, the church offers help until the widowed person can get back on his or her feet. This communal giving is always free and unconditional, and continues as long as help is needed.

The funeral and burial rites are simple; the deceased is placed in a modest pine casket and buried in a plain grave dug in a nearby Amish cemetery. A non-Amish mortician may help by embalming the corpse, but in many churches there is no such preparation. Both men and women are buried in white; married women are buried in their wedding dresses. Funerals take place three days after death, with the viewing and the service held in the house of the deceased.

The funeral service is similar to the regular church service, although the sermon and scriptures are tailored for the occasion. After the graveside service, everyone returns to the house to share in a meal and fellowship. The mourning period lasts up to a year, but Amish are encouraged to remarry, especially if widowed while still young.

Above:
Amish funerals are conducted three days after death, at the home of the deceased, and attended by friends and relatives. The service is similar to the regular church service.

Right:
Amish cemeteries are characterized by fairly plain tombstones showing only the name, birth date, and death date of the deceased. Many Amish open the casket at the cemetery for family and friends to say goodbye one last time.

CHAPTER 4

BROTHERHOOD: THE COMFORT OF COMMUNITY

Like many unique cultures, the Amish are defined not only by geographic separations and ethnic differences but also by language. Most Amish speak and read English as well as German (their Bible and the *Ausband* are written in German). However, the Amish have their own German-based dialect—Pennsylvania Dutch—that sets them apart from the rest of society and further binds them together as a community.

The name isn't derived from their country of origin—most of the Amish arrived from Switzerland, Germany, or German-speaking areas of France—but instead is an Anglicized pronunciation of the German word *Deutsche* (meaning "German"). Since the early immigrants settled in Pennsylvania, the dialect became known as Pennsylvania Dutch. This language is not unique to the Amish; many of the other groups with common Anabaptist origins also use this dialect today.

EDUCATION

The Amish have fought a long and bitter battle against the government to preserve their right to educate their own children. Until the last few decades, there was a peaceful alliance between the Amish and the public education system. Amish children attended public schools, learning the basics right beside non-Amish students; some Amish fathers were even involved with local school boards.

Unfortunately, the consolidating of the rural schools, the extending of the school year to 180 days, and the raising of the minimum age that children are required to remain in school from fourteen to sixteen threatened the very existence of the farm and the Amish way of life. The Amish contended that consolidation caused children to be bused far from home, alienating them from their families, and the lengthened school year threatened the spring planting.

More critical to the Amish way of life, mandatory attendance until age sixteen forced Amish youths to attend high school, where they were exposed to worldly ideas and beliefs foreign to their faith. They believed this could corrupt and

Left:

School usually begins at 8:00 AM and ends around 3:00 PM. Amish schools don't observe the same number of holidays that English schools do. However, during spring planting and fall harvesting, schools may have early dismissal so older children can help with the farm work.

Right:
Like their English counterparts, Amish children have special days at school. One of these is Pet Show Day. Each child brings a favorite pet to show to the class, perhaps the family dog, cat, or even a much-loved pony.

Right:
Amish children attend school through the eighth grade. Reading, writing, arithmetic, and geography are taught. Lessons are given in English so the pupils will be able to communicate with the outside world as adults.

Right:
Two boys carry lunch boxes packed with food for the midday break. Amish education is funded by families in each district. Besides supporting their own schools, the Amish pay regular school taxes just like their English neighbors.

possibly destroy the fabric of their society. Religion is woven into every corner of Amish life, including their schooling. With children attending larger schools farther away from home, Amish parents and the church were concerned that they could no longer supervise what their children were learning.

Subjects that question "why?" are taught in the high schools; the Amish are taught from an early age not to question, but to accept that which is told them. Individual achievement, competitiveness, and pride are fostered in public schools, but these concepts can be antithetical to the teachings of community, sharing, and humility. To the Amish, education should enhance what the young person needs to know as an adult, not contradict or compromise their way of life. They believe that education after the eighth grade should be the responsibility of the parents, and learning should come by example and practice, not merely from books.

The battle over the Amish child's education became heated during the 1950s and 1960s, as fathers went to jail rather than send their children to high school. The Amish were forced to resort to lawyers to present their case, a practice the Amish try to avoid at all costs as it goes against their philosophy of non-resistance. The issue was finally settled in favor of the Amish by the United States Supreme Court in 1972. The feeling of the Amish people toward education is best summed up in the words of Chief Justice Warren Burger:

> Amish objection to formal education beyond the eighth grade is firmly grounded in central religious beliefs. They object to the high school and higher education generally because the values it teaches are in marked variance with Amish values. . . . Amish society emphasizes informal learning-through-doing, a life of goodness, rather than a life of intellect; wisdom, rather than technical knowledge; community welfare, rather than competition; and separation, rather than integration with contemporary worldly society.

SCHOOLS TODAY

Across the country, one-room schoolhouses dot the Amish landscape. The schools are close enough for most students to either walk to or ride to in buggies, but in some areas where distance is a factor, vans owned by "English" drivers transport the students back and forth. These vans

Left:
Amish children attend school the mandatory number of days and hours required by the state in which they live. During the school day, the children have two recesses and a lunch break. In winter, a hill provides the perfect place for sliding in the snow.

Above:
Amish children play outside in all seasons. In winter, ice skating is a popular sport for youngsters, as well as for unmarried teens.

are licensed by the state and clearly indicate that students are aboard.

Teachers are usually unmarried Amish girls, but in some areas there are male teachers as well. The teachers usually lack any further training beyond their own eighth-grade education and they are not required to be state certified. Instead, the teacher is chosen for his or her interest in education, teaching abilities, and high moral character. Paid a moderate salary, the teacher is evaluated periodically by the parents and district in which they serve.

Religion is not taught in the schools—that is the responsibility of the church and parents—but daily scripture readings are recited and hymns are sung in music class. All lessons are taught in English, forcing the children to become fluent in the language necessary for dealing with the outside world. Pennsylvania Dutch is spoken during lunch and on the playground, but as more and more specialty words are coined in English they crop up in everyday conversation, creating an interesting mixture of the two languages.

The curriculum includes basic courses in reading, writing, arithmetic, and geography using old, discarded textbooks or, in some cases, copies of the original *McGuffey Reader*. To help shape the school curriculum and introduce some unity to schools around the country, the Old Order Book Society helps to find suitable teaching materials. Pathway Publishers, an Old Order Amish company located in Aylmer, Ontario, prints a monthly magazine for teachers, the *Blackboard Bulletin*.

In Pennsylvania, the school year is 180 days long, satisfying state education requirements, and the school day is usually from 8:00 AM to 3:00 PM. Young children learn patience while the older students are taught, and, in turn, the older children help take care of the young ones. There are usually two breaks during the day, one in the morning and one in the afternoon, and everyone brings their own lunch.

Contrary to popular belief, Amish parents pay local school taxes in addition to financing their own schools. By volunteering in the classroom, pitching in when things need to be built or repaired, and attending school picnics, parents offer support in every other aspect of their child's education as well.

Communications

Since telephone use is banned within the home and transportation is chiefly by horse and buggy, communication between family and friends can take from several days to several weeks. Word of mouth is still the principle form of communication, a practice strengthened by church services and visiting. Staying in touch with friends and family who have

Above:
Many Amish farm families have pet dogs. As companions for the younger
members of the family and as lookouts, dogs are a vital part of the farm scene.

Left:
Blacksmiths are very important within the Amish community. Caring for draft animals and the horses used to pull the family buggies, blacksmiths are kept busy. Some blacksmiths make house calls, traveling to farms in order to shoe the animals on the spot.

Left:
Auctions provide a chance for Amish men to visit. During the sale, everything from the weather to new crop techniques is discussed.

Following page:
Amish children love to roller skate. Usually, skates are used as a means of transportation, but sometimes, they are just for the fun and thrill of fast motion.

Left:
Horses are an important part of the Amish way of life. Amish and English alike attend horse auctions in order to purchase new animals for their many needs.

Left:
In many areas, a weekly livestock and produce auction is held. Using the same method as a public estate auction, an auctioneer starts the bidding for an animal at a certain price, and people continue to bid until only one buyer remains. A variety of farm animals, from horses to chickens, are sold in this way.

Left:
During the heat of summer, Amish children love to swim and play in water just like other children. A make-shift raft cut from a piece of styrofoam offers a means to float down stream.

moved away is done by letter either via the US postal service or non-Amish couriers.

There are several large-circulation publications which spread the news farther and faster than word-of-mouth or letters can. *The Budget*, published weekly in Sugar Creek, Ohio, is read by many Old Order groups as well as by more liberal Amish and Mennonites and some non-Amish people. Circulated nationally, the paper reports such items as births, marriages, deaths, natural and man-made disasters, and sales of farms and furnishings. When help is needed in a certain area to rebuild after fires or storms, the word is spread for volunteers to answer the cry for aid.

Another weekly publication, *Die Botschaft* (The Message), is published in Lancaster County, Pennsylvania, specifically for the Old Order Amish, and covers the same kind of news. There have been other publications throughout the years, but these two papers remain the vital link between the expanding Amish communities.

ACTIVITIES INSIDE THE COMMUNITY

Children of all ages and ethnic backgrounds love to play games, and Amish children are no exception. They enjoy red rover, baseball, round town (a form of baseball), and volley-

Above:

It's very hard to distinguish between Old Order Mennonites and Old Order Amish. Both dress similarly and use horses and buggies for transportation. Youth from either group enjoy picnicking and boating on local rivers and streams.

Right:

Young people of all ages and groups like to go on outings together. Unlike their Amish cousins, many of the Mennonites drive cars. These Mennonite teenagers have traveled to a nearby river to cool their feet on a hot summer day.

ball. Games are played at school, after church and after weddings, or just when someone comes to visit.

Some men play board games like chess or checkers, but the main form of interaction between community members is visiting. Through this simple act, the Amish people stay close to their roots. Interacting with those of the same beliefs, they reinforce the strong bonds of tradition and family and form a mutual-aid society within a community of righteous individuals.

Visiting isn't always conducted in a formal manner, such as after a church or funeral service. A group may travel together to a garden or a zoo, hiring a taxi driver to allow more time to visit while traveling. Special occasions such as birthday parties, picnics, and family reunions bring family and friends together.

"Sisters Days" bring women together as they share the work of cleaning or canning vegetables and fruits. Quilting circles not only create beautiful articles of bedding, but also allow women the time to talk and share in a relaxed atmosphere. Business and pleasure may be mixed at public auctions, as well as on market days when people from several areas meet to sell their excess produce, jams, jellies, baked goods, and craft items.

Two unique activities that not only bring people together but also display the true meaning of giving freely and helping those in need are work "frolics" and barn raisings. Frolics can be organized by anyone and may be announced at church, at other social gatherings, or simply by word of mouth as people meet in shops or on the road. A frolic can be called to help build a new shed, to repair or paint an existing building, or to finish some last-minute work in the fields. The sponsoring host not only provides the work to be done, but also treats all of those helping to sumptuous food and sometimes, especially when young people are involved, an opportunity to have a social gathering at the end of the work.

A barn raising is truly one of the most remarkable enterprises one could hope to witness. Usually scheduled after a disaster has destroyed an Amish barn, this one-day phenomenon displays how the power of an entire community can come to the aid of one family in need. Prior to the barn raising friends and family gather to help clean up the mess, which in the case of a fire entails removing burnt carcasses (if any livestock were lost), burnt wood, hay, and farm machinery, and repairing the foundation of the barn.

On the day of the raising, the Amish men and women—and in some cases several non-Amish folks—gather at the farm. Without a foreman, everyone cooperates and, by day's end, the group of men and boys has erected an entire barn. The women are just as important behind the scenes, preparing enormous quantities of food for the noontime meal and offering snacks to keep the workers going through the day. It's a hard day, but the satisfaction gained by helping others can never be replaced.

Left:
Amish life is very hard. Children of all ages have certain chores to perform, including caring for younger brothers and sisters. Sometimes, when all of their duties are completed, they head to a nearby hill for wagon riding.

Right:
Children of all ages
love to play on swings.
On the playground or
at home, Pennsylvania
Dutch is spoken. The early
Amish settlers spoke this
German-based dialect when
they arrived in America.

Right:
During the warmer months,
Amish children and adults
rarely wear shoes. Whether
at play or at work, many
Amish prefer to go barefoot,
even during a baseball game
that uses rocks as bases.

Right:
Retired people of all faiths head south for the winter. There are many different church-run retirement
communities scattered throughout the southern states. Some of these resorts are operated by Mennonites.
It's not uncommon to find Amish retirees enjoying a game of shuffleboard at one of these communities.

Right:
When funds are needed to aid a member of their church, the Amish have a benefit sale. All items are donated and all proceeds are given to the needy family.

Below:
In 1992, an arsonist destroyed six Amish barns in the Big Valley area of central Pennsylvania. Financial aid came from around the world to help rebuild the barns and to replace lost animals and equipment.

In March of 1992, six Amish barns in the Big Valley area of central Pennsylvania were destroyed by arson. The outpouring of good will—in the form of financial contributions and manpower—that was directed toward this small Amish enclave from around the world renewed the community's faith in mankind.

A special trust fund was set up at a local bank to help pay for the replacement of the farm animals and equipment lost in the fires, and volunteers of all faiths and persuasions descended into the valley to help with the clean-up and rebuilding. Within a month, all of the barns were rebuilt; most were erected within a one-week span. The farmers could once again resume their work, milking the new herds and using the new equipment and draft animals supplied

by friends that they may never have the opportunity to meet again.

RELIEF WORK

In some communities, the Amish volunteer in fire and emergency companies, services that strengthen the bonds between the Amish and their "English" neighbors. Although the Amish are always available to help members of their own community in times of death, ill health, and natural or man-made disasters, they often extend this aid to non-Amish neighbors as well. Among their own people, many support such special funds as the Amish Aid Society; begun in the latter part of the 1800s, this form of insurance is supported by a "fire tax" that helps defray its members' losses due to fire and

Above:
When a shed needs to be built or repaired, an Amishman sends out word to
his neighbors and schedules a work "frolic." The frolic usually lasts only a single
day but during this time, an entire barn roof may be laid or a new shed built.

Left:
Women play an important role during a barn raising. Although they are in the background, their job is vital. To supply the workers with snacks and a good home-cooked meal, mountains of food must be prepared. The work, and the feast that follows, provides a welcome time of enjoyment and relaxation for everyone involved.

Right:
A barn raising is an exciting experience. In one day's time, an entire barn will be raised, or built, by a group of men and boys. If the project is a large one, "English" neighbors, as well as other Amish, may join in the task.

Below:
A barn raising takes many men and boys. Working as a team, the group assembles the barn from the side supports to the roof in just one day.

storm damage. The church also acts as a relief service, coming to its members' aid when financial problems threaten the family farm or when chores need attending to in times of death and illness.

The Amish also cooperate with their Mennonite brethren in two charitable world-wide organizations. To the Mennonite Central Committee, the Amish donate dry goods such as clothing and bedding and volunteer their time for such activities as meat canning (to be distributed to the world's hungry). Quilts, crafts, and baked goods are also donated to be auctioned off to raise money for the committee's projects.

Other Amish groups support the Mennonite Disaster Service, a relief organization analogous to the more familiar American Red Cross. During times of floods, hurricanes, or other natural disasters, crews of Amish join their Mennonite brethren throughout North America, helping in the clean-up and rebuilding of devastated areas.

Above:
A newly-built barn is a marvel to behold, and in just one day, a farmer hit by a
man-made or natural disaster can be back on his feet in a very short period of time.

CHAPTER 5
THE TEMPTATIONS OF MODERN LIFE

In the eastern United States, many Amish communities are surrounded by modern urban populations with all the latest technology. Despite the financial interdependence of the Amish and their more contemporary neighbors, the gap between these two cultures continues to widen. Innovative Amish have adapted modern equipment, both on their farms and in their shops, enabling both the farmer and businessman to stay competitive while following the strict rules of the *Ordnung*. Although the older generations are secure with their identities and relationships to the church and community, for members of the younger generation the lure of the modern world at times can be too great to ignore.

SOWING WILD OATS

Near heavily urbanized areas such as Lancaster County, Pennsylvania, it's not unusual to see Amish youth "cruising" on a Sunday in buggies festooned with plush carpet interiors and large dice or other adornments hanging from the windshields, and with boom boxes blaring rock music. The boys may be wearing baseball uniforms as they head to local league games. You can find youths hanging out at local convenience stores or you might be shocked to see young Amishmen out on the town on Saturday night, driving flashy cars, drinking beer, or taking in the sights.

Rumors of rowdy parties of Amish adolescents have long been circulated among the "English." These parties, held at a barn or a rented hall, provide the young people with a vehicle to let loose and taste the forbidden pleasures of dancing and drinking. There are reported cases of drunkenness and other mischievous conduct; unfortunately, some of these incidents have led to vehicular accidents and death.

When an Amish friend was questioned about this sowing of wild oats, he replied, "If you don't let them try it and get it out

Right:
Amish youth "sow the wild oats" during their teenage years. Driving cars, attending parties, and drinking alcoholic beverages occurs more frequently than some Amish would like to admit. But strong church and family ties usually bring the adventurers back into the community by the time they are ready for communion and marriage.

Left:
Young boys share in farm work from an early age. Learning the skills required to be good farmers is important to them. By the time a young man is married, this knowledge must be second nature so that he, too, can run his own farm.

Left:
On this Amish farm in Ohio, as in many areas, the house and yard are immaculate. Clothes hanging on the line to dry are a common sight, especially on a sunny day.

Left:
Amish women wear their uncut hair pulled back into a tight bun at the base of the neck. Following the Scriptures as written in I Corinthians 11, women always have their heads covered.

Right:
The inside of the Amish home is very simple, without pictures, mirrors, or other decorations. Each room is neat, with a place for everything.

Right:
On many Amish farms attractive flower beds can be seen around the house and barnyard. Amish women have a green thumb for growing flowers and vegetables. However, some sects, such as the Nebraska Amish, prefer their homes less adorned, and do not grow flowers.

Right:
Thrashing oats for horse feed is hard work even when it's not done by hand. When an Amishman's crop is ready, several farmers come together to accomplish the task. With more hands helping, the job is not only done much faster, but the important sense of community is also reinforced.

of their systems, then they may always wonder what it is like on the other side. Eventually, some might leave the church entirely." In fact, many of the boys who go through this wild time aren't yet members of the church—they have not yet been baptized; when they do become members, they often-times make the best leaders. Girls usually join the church at a younger age than boys, so one never sees a young Amish woman driving a car or sitting in a bar.

During the critical formative years of childhood and early adulthood, the Amish society teaches young people the values of community and adherence to the *Ordnung*; everything the child experiences channels his or her thinking and behavior toward one day being a willing member of this fellowship. Even if a young person experiences a "wild" time, it's difficult for him or her to leave something that is familiar and safe. These strong community ties usually bring the errant individual back home.

The New Order and Old Order Amish treat the youth very differently during these formative years. Many Old Order groups look the other way as their young people wander, but the New Order Amish, in contrast to their stricter neighbors, have established youth groups. These organizations provide a chaperoned environment where young people can socialize within the confines of the church community.

EXCOMMUNICATION AND SHUNNING

Sometimes a wayward person cannot make the extreme sacrifices that are demanded of them by tradition and culture—modern conveniences pose too much of a temptation. When these infractions come to the attention of the church and bishop, sanctions against the person or people are sometimes imposed. In extreme cases, the *bann*, or act of excommunication, is announced. Along with excommunication comes *meidung*, the shunning from communion and fellowship.

Meidung can be a tormenting, severe punishment; indeed, it was this harshness which prompted Ammann to split from the Swiss Anabaptists in 1693. Shunning is a most effective

Left:
Amish children often accompany their mother on errands to town. Amish mothers rarely need a baby-sitter as their young are usually well behaved no matter where they are taken. If the child gets a little out of hand, a stern look from the mother is all it takes to restore calm.

Above:
In Ontario, Canada, an Amish woman sells her goods at a weekly farmer's market. Children often accompany their mothers to market, helping behind the counter with sales of the family's products.

form of social control. Although it is a means of punishment, it is meant not to separate the individual but to unite the community; to guarantee the survival of the society, the church must quickly control any breach in established protocol and doctrine. It is believed that by letting the excommunicated experience isolation from church, community, and sometimes family, the sinful will reflect upon and amend their ways, and reenter the brotherhood of God expunged of guilt.

Except in the case of such unforgivable transgressions as owning a car or seeking a divorce, excommunication is not an immediate action; there are several steps involved in a *bann*. First the person is given a private warning, followed by a public one if the first isn't heeded. At this time, the bishop may order the person to give a confession in front of the church members. If the sinner ignores these directives a six-week *bann* is issued.

During this trial period, the errant individual is excluded from communion and the fellowship of church, and other church members—including spouse and family—are not permitted to eat at the same table as the shunned. At the end of the six weeks, the person has a choice: summoned to the church, he or she either appears and delivers a confession in front of the assembly or simply doesn't show up, further demonstrating disregard for the church and community. When the latter occurs the bishop usually decrees a final *bann*, forbidding all church members to associate with the shunned individual, both socially and commercially; husbands or wives are even instructed to cease sexual relations with a shunned spouse. In some sects, all communication and contact is severed between the individual and the community.

Above:
In Strasburg, Pennsylvania, not only can tourists tour a working Amish farm, but they can also ride an authentic steam railroad and visit a toy train museum. Another attraction is the Red Caboose Motel where one can stay overnight in a real train caboose.

Left:
Many people travel to Amish country to sample a variety of delectable food items available from various vendors. Amish women excel at creating baked goods that cause even the casual shopper's mouth to water.

TOURISM

The outside world has always been fascinated by the Amish but with the release of motion pictures like *Witness*, the popularity of the Amish skyrocketed. This movie centered on the life of one character, a young Amish widow (played by Kelly McGillis), and the disruption of her life by a Philadelphia detective (Harrison Ford). Filmed on location in Lancaster County, the movie caused quite a furor among the local Amish.

The filming was upsetting to the community on several fronts. It challenged their doctrines against television and photography in their lives, while exposing them to the world's scrutiny even as they, as a people, avoided all publicity. Most tragic, perhaps, is that the Amish realized they were being exploited, not only by the film company but also by the local and state tourist bureaus. One scene—in which Ford, dressed in plain clothes, defends the Amish in a fist fight—was particularly offensive, directly contradicting their treasured

Right:
Many of the older Amish men practice woodworking after they leave the farm. Smaller pieces, like these birdhouses, are popular with tourists visiting Amish country.

Left:
Whether they are part of the Nebraska sect, Beachy sect, or another Old Order group, Amish people in general are fine craftsmen. This Beachy Amish woman puts the final touches on a handmade stool.

Right:
Traditional Amish crafts, such as this chair and doll, draw tourists from all over the world to the Amish countryside.

OUT OF THE PAST

OUT OF THE PAST

OUT OF THE PAST

Right:
Throughout the Amish areas, many fine restaurants have been established which boast home-made Pennsylvania Dutch cooking. Many of these eateries have Amish and Mennonite women in the kitchens preparing the food.

Below:
There are many designs used in quilt making. The double wedding ring and the log cabin designs are just two of the many patterns used to combine the many patches of color.

Above:
Amish women supplement the family's income by selling their surplus canned goods, fresh vegetables, and baked goods at local farmers' markets. Such items as pickled eggs and red beets, home-made relishes and pickles, and fresh fruit pies are always a favorite with the weekly shopper.

Above:
Individuality and pride are discouraged among the Amish, but women can
still excel through their skills in designing quilts. Many of the smaller squares in
the quilts are remnants of cloth left over from making the family's clothing.

principle of nonresistance. Without either aid or advice from the Amish community, *Witness* was completed and released. Later, legislation was enacted in Pennsylvania to protect the Amish from similar ventures in the future.

The influence of tourism on an area is a double-edged sword, bringing both benefits and problems. Quite rightly, it is despised by some and welcomed by others. Unfortunately, the increase in tourist-supported businesses such as motels and restaurants takes away precious farmland, sometimes displacing some of this country's most fertile ground with asphalt or cement.

Fortunately, growing interest on the part of the non-Amish in the Amish's finely crafted furniture, quilts, and delicious food has opened up business opportunities where none existed before. As farmland has grown scarce, more and more Amish have had to seek work away from home; in many cases, however, tourism-related occupations allow the Amish to remain on the farm or in the home as they work to supply the ever-growing demand for their goods.

Still, the Amish would be just as happy to be left alone to live their lives in solitude and community harmony. In fact, entire Amish communities have left some areas in search of more and cheaper land and to provide a greater buffer zone separating them from the outside world. In contrast to the hustle and bustle of tourist-rich areas like Lancaster, there are many other places in the country where the Amish still live a life of comparative peacefulness, shielded from the scrutiny of the curious onlooker.

SURVIVAL OF THE AMISH

Since the advent of electricity and automobiles, the survival of the Amish has been in jeopardy; modern technology and

Below:
Quilts are considered fine pieces of art by many people. Several places, such as the Quilt Museum in Lancaster County, Pennsylvania, have been established to showcase both past and present quilt work.

Left:
Quilting circles bring women together for a time of friendly socializing. A good quilter is judged by the length of the stitch and the even spaces between stitches.

Following page:
Throughout the Amish countryside, colorful town names exist. Blue Ball, Bird-In-Hand, Paradise, and Intercourse are among the more unusual town names found in Lancaster County, Pennsylvania.

associated ideas threaten the very essence of their society. However, with their resistance to change in certain respects and their flexibility in others, their numbers have actually doubled during the twentieth century. Still, to strive to be perfect in an imperfect world is very difficult, and the boundaries between the Amish and the outside world are constantly being redefined.

The Amish are a dynamic people, adapting to meet the demands placed on them by a world caught up in a rush, a world full of gadgets and short cuts, a world of individuals who have seemingly forgotten the meaning of togetherness. As technology advances and conveniences become day-to-day necessities, compromise is inevitable. Many Amish concessions to the modern world may appear hypocritical. However, ironically, having been forced to conform somewhat in order to maintain their separatism from the

rest of society, the Amish have successfully preserved their heritage and traditions.

As a people of God, the Amish constantly demonstrate the importance of strong faith, both in the teachings of the Scriptures and in their practice of brotherhood. Their strong adherence to a life of discipline, sacrifice, and humility binds the Amish together, while fostering a feeling of acceptance and community. The delicate balance between traditional values and modern influences has been maintained despite the occasional upheavals. The Amish offer all of us a glimpse of how a peaceful society can sustain itself amidst the violence, death, and destruction so common to our modern world. These remarkable people have survived and will continue to prosper and, perhaps, because of them the world may be a somewhat better place in which to live.

Left:
Many Amish women have been forced to work outside the home. As an alternative, the roadside stand located at the house provides women an opportunity to help the family income while staying at home where their main obligations lie.

Above:
The Amish are self-sufficient in many areas, but some things must be purchased at the nearby general store. This store in Intercourse, Pennsylvania, was used in the movie *Witness* for one of the scenes.

Right:
Amish families aren't opposed to using services provided by local banks. It's not uncommon to pull up to a drive-in window in some areas and see a buggy waiting in line, too.

Right:
A number of Amish have been forced to seek a profession away from the farm. Cabinet making and woodworking are two preferred professions. Some Amish have perfected their skills to a fine art and are considered master craftsmen in furniture and clock design.

Right:
Water on the farm is obtained in a variety of ways: hand pumps, windmills, gravity-fed springs, water-wheels, water rams, and gasoline or diesel pumps inside wells. Most Amish farms are distinguished from their "English" neighbors by the absence of electrical wires leading to the farm and by the presence of a windmill.

Right:
The juxtaposition of a high-tension power line to the natural calm of the Amish countryside is common in some areas. The encroachment of urban development into the peaceful landscape has forced some Amish communities to leave their homes in search of larger and cheaper tracts of land.

INDEX